Breaking Silence 5

Rohit Shetty

Breaking Silence 5

Rohit Shetty

First Step Publishing
Paving Ways For New Writers

First Published in 2020 by First Step Publishing
Editorial / Sales / Marketing Office at
303-304 Garnet Nirmal Lifestyles Ph 2
Behind Nirmal Lifestyles Mall
LBS Marg Mulund West
Mumbai 400080
E-Mail:- info@firststepcorp.com
www.firststepcorp.com

ISBN:- 978-93-83306-57-2
Cover Designed by: Design Fishing

Table Of Content

No more words to say

No more words to say
Even if I have to, I may?
You say you need more time
Now my words to you are
Not worth a dime
So many words to say
I may say not, or I may?

No more words to say
Even if I have to, I may?
Once gone it's difficult to bring back
The Trust which I had, with your words,
Is broken with a snap
So many words to say
I may say not, or I may?

No more words to say
Even if I have to, I may?
You say that you don't trust,
It came to me like a shock, but
For a relationship that's a must,
So many words to say
I may say not, or I may?

No more words to say
Even if I have to, I may?
Atleast I'am happy that you gave a thought,

Being true to yourself and me
I might still have a shot.
So many words to say
I may say not, or I may?

So many words to say
I may say not, or I may?
With our endless conversations and chats
All we do is fight like
Mere dogs and cats
It's all cos of your assumptions

21/12/2013

11th is the date

11th is the date
For which i just can't wait
For a friend who stays miles apart
Is coming home, who has a place in my heart

Studied together, we didn't speak much
Then years passed by, without any touch
Being neighbours though we never met
In different cities our fates were set.

We met, years later, mere coincidence
Numbers exchanged though, but never called
Staying so close we never met,
Didn't know what our fates had already set.

Talks, started from minutes
Continued to hours
It had no limits, the bond grew stronger
What once was a bud, had blossomed into a flower

You found in me the lost trust
This hand, that holds the pen,
Has many a hundred times been dust
Forgotten Him, cheated Him, Painted illusions of lust.

Nevertheless, Annihilating all that's made
To a green Thought in a green Shade.
With a gift, Me and You

I don't know how can this be true.

You call me again and again
To the place you stay miles apart.
But this time 11th is the date
For which i can't just wait.

1-7-14

Emotions

I have a smile
That runs along miles
You can see it on my face
Since the day you were at my place

I say 11th is the day
So do your friends with a smirk
You need not keep explaining to them
That's not your work

From me I'am sure, now,
You are not afraid
With you, in the ups and down, a vow i keep
You have a friend, who will not go or leave,

I gave you a hug so did you
Neither let each other go,
There was a tear in your eye
With a kiss we bade goodbye

11/7/14

Precious Moments

Nothing new, my days were without shine
I met you for a brief moment, felt you will be mine
I felt, may be, love could blossom someday
But never knew, he will take you from me, so soon away.

My heart stopped, felt as a last breath
Life cheated me again it seems
To hold your hand I yearn
But now you are someone else's, never to be mine again

Infact you were never mine
There Flew no sparks though
Can't forget the day when i first saw you
16th Feb 2014 in my calendar it marks though.

Had seen your photos many times,
Heard about you as well,
Wanting to meet you, tried hard
Sunday it was, but, my feelings I couldn't tell.

The stars, it seems are not in my favour
Without you, I will live forever free
May be it's my work I shall marry to.
It reminds me of my credentials, ME!

For now, I won't be waiting for you
Deprived of precious moments
Without any clue.

16/7/14

Lust

Lust, that's the name,
Is Love lust, or it's the same
Love is from the heart
Many say, and believe it's true
Lust, Only a desire
Understood by few.

Love an emotional things
That one can feel
Lust, not the binding factor
Though, has its own appeal.

Lust, a desire
i believe is true
Lust, not same as love
That's all i'am saying to you.

Which emotion you feel
Love, or lust my friend
Its important to understand the difference
Or relations will eventually end

If you love her....tell her so,
This I beg of you,
Or If it's lust your after,
Let her know it, try to be true.

One thing I have eventually learned,

in this post teen age of mine,
Sex is not what makes a relationship,
But love, faith and honesty, it's divine!

29/7/14

Let me share a story

I picked a nobody
Made her a somebody
She stabbed me in my back
With great precision and knack

What do I do now
I don't know
Will now remove her name
What disgrace that will be and shame

I wished to see the reaction
On her face
Its cos of her own actions
She has landed herself in this maze

Money lost, so did some name
Lesson learnt the hard way
Now she has no rights, no claim
i have shoved her for good, far away.

Often my Dad says
Share your space with people of same rank
Should have heeded his advice i feel now
His experience is nothing less than a treasure bank.

I don't mind spending more
To teach her a lesson
She shall fret full sore. 30/7/14

Lets talks about my roommates

Prajna, the caretaker at home
She's proud, but she needs to roam
To learn cutlery skills
Before anybody needs to pop a pill

Chris, tall with long legs
The only one, who can lift me up
Holding me like a tea cup

Anu, The girl with a single colour
Maroon it is,
It has no sister or any brother

Geetika, The bodybuilder
Goes on many blind dates
globing up with many plates

Sharmi, the sale girl,
She want it at the price of a banana
That expensive pearl

An here am i, Mittali
Once as I told in glee
Tales of the stormy sea.

12/8/14

Comedy Miles

Miles apart we stay
So many things, yet to say
Can't forget your scream
Amazed, you thought, you were in a dream

Now, for hours we talk
In every call, i gave you
Atleast two or three shocks

Coming back to you
Camera i say is there
Searching your eyes everywhere

Your laughter seems funny
Whenever I mimic
Holding your stomach, paining with laughter
All you say, that's enough honey.

Lizard ! I exclaim, on your wall
Jumping to find where
Everytime you almost fall

Sometimes I'm in the mood,
I wanna back up against the wall
Sometimes you are in the mood,
You wanna run away, still you can't crawl

It gets funny at times
Being a person full of colours
You keep searching where the hell are the shutters.
All the time looking for cover.

Your laughter seems losing a volume
Since the day, she has flown in, in maroon
God only knows, where she has come from
Is it from mars or probably the moon?

Losing a bet, you asked me my prize
Calmly I said its Samsung galaxy S5
I don’t know when will it arrive
All i can do is just strive.

You keep saying to me
All the time with a smirk
That nothing can be done
To make your mind work

It all started with
Hunting a bride for me
Eventually a groom for you.
Landed being a Stepney to each other with no clue.

Most importantly you throw
Tantrums while eating food
When hungry you eat little
Trying to make a fool of me, That’s very rude.

Still i catch you
Sitting miles apart
So many things to say
Thoughts that draws us heart to heart.

12/8/14

Smile

A smile is something that has lost from my face
From the whirlwind of time and its maze

i want to smile, but i don't know i cant
is it because of the seeds, that i had plant

i know iam true to time with its struggles apart
Money has come between, the hope of my heart

i want to smile, i don't know when will that be
A space, redeemed from toil and care,
From tears and sadness, i want to be free.

May be peace i will find when i rest in my grave
Who knows, i will be treated even there as a slave

But still there is something missing on my face
Its a smile, a smile, wondered on a far off place.

28/8/14

Together again

Together again
To be with you
How would i know
Seconds would be few

Yet another
Day had passed
Raining, lightning
Gloomy weather had cast

Miles apart
Thinking of you
It's not the distance,
Distance, there in the heart.

Maybe someday
Time will come
To be together
Or forever be Apart

May be
Today is the day
I, can't unwind the screw
Time changed, with the morning dew

Forever together
Being miles apart
How could I think?

I still have no clue

But now
Dust has settled
Grass, shining with morning dew
Making the day, fresh and new.

1/11/14

Success

Roads are many to choose
I chose the one who dared a few
I stumbled, i fell,
And now an indiscrete tale i tell

Success is a metaphor
It's Where things that own not man's dominion dwell,
It's like a surging wave
Where sailing ships sinks in the swell.

Yet I tried to conquer the waves
Not knowing the fact, where the waves are taking me
I stood by, strong and brave
It was a time when no one stood for thee.

Days passed by, so did months
Years it took,
Stead of learning' to live i was learning to die.
Suddenly i had my soul's unchanging look;

I worked on the island,
Manned by none, or few i knew
I'll make you smile, rather buy you diamonds
Well I try to get closer but I'm still a million miles from you
I ain't bluffing, seriously, iam true.

Untrodden is the path i'am walking on
While other start slipping and in no time they are gone
Here am i standing in success
I learned from No, so much more than from a yes.

1/12/14

Distance Apart Miles.

It feels great
When you make someone smile
Who is apart from miles
But the one who is miles apart
Comes close,
What do you call it fate.

I am walking on a sword sharp
One mistake, it will slit me apart
Been here a time not so long ago
To build lost trust
Is like Walking on
A mountain all covered with snow.

My silence speaks for me
But here I would love to speak
To open my mind with you
And scream in silence
Life can it be so bleak.

Well here i am
And there you are
Will be with you, though miles apart
Making you smile
With distance apart miles.

4/1/15

Yes, i crave for you

Yes, i crave for you
the laughs we shared
the times we spent
Were very few

Had it had to end this way
perhaps i didn't have a clue
Minor misunderstanding,
All i wanted was, To just be with you

Time passed, Years gone
Life moved on, struggling along
But here iam, standing in success
A dream, turned to reality,
At the break of dawn.

A decade passed by
Where are you, I have no clue
It was you, turned to we
Never meant for I, but it had to be.

A Decade apart
With countless miles
Yes i still crave for you
Cos time spent with you
Were elite and few.

6/1/14

Emotions

I have a smile today with a tear in my eye
Smile for meeting a friend after years
And tear for saying a friend goodbye

I don't know what's wrong with me
A medley of emotions running amok
I feel it's the smile, that's never meant to be.
Or the tears .

13/7/14

Poetry

Reading my diary
Flipping its pages
I realised one thing
I haven't written from ages.

Finding its reasons
Contemplating on thoughts
Answers i couldn't find
Nothing in my mind came across

Then i found
The dried ink
Like the love gone away
Contemplating again i sat to think

The pen had no refill then
And you came across
Like a cold wind in summers
Sweet, yet spicer than a hot sauce.

I found the ink
Like it seemed to me
Flowing like a verse
Smooth and free

A soiled page
Is Now i have
Soiled with ink, and poetry
I write as I grace the stage

14/2/15

Untitled

Rose, When faded
Memories Dwell on
Beauty Shadowed
Her sweet smell gone

Vanishing loveliness
Burdening beneath
Craving not for her then
Its the battle encircling wreath,

Immortal Thought
Whose passion Still
Makes the changing
The Unchangeable

Oh, thus thy beauty
Gorgeous on earth, to me
Bright with sorrows, shines
And Burns with me.

20/2/15

Cast Away

Do i miss you now
No i don't
For the place in my heart
Is now vacant
Which was occupied by you

Did i shed a tear
No i didn't
Though the pain in my heart
Severe and Gruelling
We, now are distance apart

Did i move on
Yes I did
For this was bound to happen
Had read your heart long back
Your love is your radiant passion

I will not stop writing
Will write till i may
For there is now no one in my life
To hold on to
Else i will just cast away

22/2/15

Days Changes

A new beginning awaits me
A new dawn in horizon
Never wished that the day will change
But days change, it’s for a reason

Love, begin’d with a spark
Continued its flames
Now extinguished in ashes
Laughing and crying - Nothing remains

For all i feel now is like a mere pawn
In the game of chess
Sacrificed for kings and queens
Now culminating my own mess

Alas! its for you, a friend you have lost
Teaching him a lesson, never trust again
May be its the pen i hold now
Iam jotting it down, the day has changed
Watered with last night's rain.

1/3/15

Words has its own imprint.

If i say i'am sad i will tell you
But you need to be that close
Else i ain't saying a word
That maybe you said or maybe you heard

Being an open book, it harms
Rather being closed, suffocates
So you need to be cautious now
Who can read, the book, you allow.

Well mine is closed, for good
As earlier written, threw it as hard as i could
Never to be found again
It would be found, i aint wondering, when?

For chapters in your novel
You can re-write, mistakes, can be changed
But wounds, last forever,
Words has its own imprint.

2/3/15

Antonyms

Its nothing more
That I want to see
Or nothing less
That i can't

It's the truth
that I want to hear
Not the lie
They you fear.

4/3/15

Reasons i don't Know

I asked you why
For the reasons i don't know
Unanswered are the questions
That i should and want to know

Your silence speaks nothing
Neither it screams, as you feel
Unanswered are the questions
Reasons i don't know.

You can still set things right
All you need to say, is a sorry
But that alone won't help you
Answers, i need, which i don't know.

Reducing calls, messages and chats,
Won't do any good to you
Chances slender, going more slim
You need to answer, Answer
The reasons, that i still don't know.

8/3/15

Answer

I want to know the answer
I was asked
Had taken too long to contemplate
It's high time and she can't wait.

I have answered my answer
Asked some time ago
Decision had to be and has been taken
Answer, whatever, she must know.

Sooner or later, better sooner now
The whistle will and has to blow
The answer is Yes, and not a No
And i did let her know.

9/3/15

Amidst

Amidst some rising stars
Embossing my legacy
Forward i move
Towards my rising glory

Amidst the critics
Trying to pull me down
Now standing in success
I dont see them around

Amidst all the mess
Lying, is nothing but paper around
A book i strive to write
Capturing silence, with its strange sound.

I yearn to write
And I write to earn
Amidts life's hustle,
I live, and i learn.

Here i am now, and there you are
Never imagined, crossroads exists
Through the thick and thin
I am driving my way,
Through this thin mist.

17/4/15

Feelings

Some notes must never be sung
Some Chords must never be struck
Some tunes should be left untouched
Some words should be left unsaid

Words are less, to express
The emotions, unheard, just felt
Writing verses and rhymes
Trying to emote the feelings felt.

Say less, Feel the emotions, they say
How to feel? When emotions are left unsaid.
To say or not to say the emotions you feel,
Say it! As no one knows what lies ahead

Expressed my emotions, result unknown
Screaming silence, through blinding night
Yes or no!, Outcome, i don't know.
Answer, awaited with morning light.

Now, Iam
Singing the perfect tune
Striking the right chords
Melodious the tune now
Saying the words that had to be said.

24/4/15

Life

Unknown people bringing a smile
While, known brings a tear
Is it life, as it seems
Or seems, that its life.

Many say, clear words
Many don't, leaves them unclear
Some scream in silence,
While, silence, screams back at them.

To be or not to be,
Is the golden question.
Many ask why? While i say this,
I see a silver lining in the sky.

Life is present in abundance,
Or, absent in scarcity.
Deny now, Accept later
Life is about, having the right flavour.

29/4/15

Relations Worth a dime.

Mind You, Mind Me,
The words you need to mind
In this commercial world
Its money that you need to mind

Relations turned sour
Mind you it's not words
Its money that plays its role
Its heartless, beats without a soul

Even to begin a new relation
It's not the qualities of a boy
that's been asked, It's his worth
At present, not of future, or past.

Awesome relations turned sour,
It's all cos of a dime,
Like an old fashioned story book
With no reason or rhyme.

Its the phase where you have lost everything and the relations turned sour. it's when you have no money in your pockets. People turn hostile, turn away from you, all because you have no money with you.
Indeed it's a commercial world. Many a times i feel like this world is not for me, or i don't belong here, death is all i wish for, for i have no reason to be alive. Then i think of my parents. They have aspirations for me

though no money, its on a hope we are alive. with creditors on our head.

25/5/15

Love and Waves

I will not wait
For the one,
Who does not wish to come
It's not because of time
Probably it's now too late

I will not cry
For my tears have dried
Its money or love, Or
Love for money
That you can't hide.

I will not smile
For i aint an artist
Performing Mime, Lonely Though
Throughout the Time

I will not speak,
A single word,
For i have said a lot before,
My love will be like a beach
Where waves breaks upon the shore.

25/5/15

Words

It takes the whole ocean
And the moon to erase
Your mere footsteps on sand

It takes just a few words
Little misunderstandings
To tear up the relation one has

It takes the earth And the Sun
Working continuously
To create days and night

But it just takes a few words to say
You are not the masterpiece
You are mere a painter too.

28/1/15

Distances

I had you then,
Who yearned to listen to my poems
As i wrote them along
Through the distance there with miles then
Now you don't even speak to me
Though the distance remains the same in miles
Its the rift in the heart, that's stolen
Our laughs and smiles

I don't know now
Whom to blame for it,
May be its money Distance, or Time,
Or combination of all, But its now the
Distance created in the heart, which
Cant be measured in miles, Or time in seconds
Or Money by its dimes.

Distances blur then
But clear now with miles apart
I had warned you once, Don't go far
So away that you can't come back even if you wished
Keep the distance measured, through the lines you
drew
But now those lines, created a rift,
With such a distance, That can't be scaled,
Even If wished to.

25/5/15

Poet and Poetry

I'am not a poet
Yet i write poetry
Words flows with emotions
Emotions turns to poetry

I just take some time
Rather stolen from myself
Or, for the ones i love
To write, and get lost in myself

Like the Melancholy
In a painters painting,
Created with strokes of brush
Poetry, i create, with strokes of pen

Yet i'am not a poet
I write, i frame emotions
To words, and create a verse
May be its a gift, or a curse.

4/6/15

Distances

It's in your loneliness
That i would be remembered
But the fact would be then
I would have gone too far

The distance can't be measured by miles then
Because the distance is created in my heart
Tried a lot to avoid it
But destiny, you call fate
Had played its role
Creating distances in miles first
And then creating it in my heart

I wouldn't love anyone now
For it takes more than it gives
I should have known this
Forgot it, i don't know how?

10/6/15

When I see you again

It's been a long day
Without you my friend
And i will tell you all about it
When i see you again

We have come a long way
From where we would get back
Oh i will tell you all about it
When i see you again.

The bond will never be broken
The love would never be lost
Though a line had to be drawn
As we had come a long way
From where we could get back
I will tell you all about it
When i see you again.

The line now it's drawn
It's a point to remember
That we had come too far
Now is the time we meet
And i'am telling you all again.

11/7/15

Antonyms

Options are many
Choices are few
To be with you
Seriously, no clue

Again you came
Again you went
Without meeting me
Had i been too far to flee.

Then Days were less
Now Days were many
Thy angry flames meant me,
Retort on thee:

Speaking more then
Speaking less now
I aint a toy with a switch
Don't hope for an another hitch

Closer you are
Though miles apart
Let not this silence
Create distances in heart

14/1/15

Innocent Love

He:
What have I said to you, my love,
To cause such pain and agony?
My precious, tender, lovely dove,
This question haunts me endlessly.

Or, is it something I have done
In ignorance or in foolish pride?
'This you I love and you, alone,
So give the answer, do not hide.

She:
Dearest one, I am in pain- -
My heart near bursts with agony.
Will ever I see my love, again?
Is the thought which brings the pain to me.

'Tis not something that you have said,
Nor some bad thing that you have done,
The thought of losing you, I dread;
I, too, love you and you alone.

He:
My sweet, my lovely spring borne flower,
What brings this though to trouble you?
Let's brush away the mist this hour.
I cannot bear to see you blue.

She:
I travel now to a distant land.
While I'm there, will our love grow cold?
My darling, take and hold my hand,
My love, more precious than jewels or gold.

How long? The answer I know not,
Perhaps a year, or two, or more.
How lonely am I at the very thought.
What does tomorrow hold in store?

My parents think it best I go
And live with them on that distant shore.
How can I bear it? I do not know.
Why must I leave the one whom I adore.

He:
My darling, sweet and precious thing,
I now can understand your pain.
While you were here I felt like a king,
But, I'm sure we'll meet again.

For you to remain would seem like heaven,
But, perhaps it's better that we wait,
Seeing you are not yet seven
And I have just turned eight.

6/1/16

Unsaid

There are so many things
People need to say,
But they just let it go
Until it's too late.
So many words unspoken,
And never get heard,
Too afraid of the pain,
Too afraid to get hurt.

Feelings kept,
Deep down inside,
Locked away with
Foolish pride.
Never knowing
What their tomorrow may hold,
And still too stubborn
to just let go.

So, I'm not
Going to wait!
Win, Loose, or Draw,
I'm letting it go,
I'm telling you it all!
You are Everything
I could dream of,
And so much more,
You are the key to my every closed door.
You are Everything,

I could dream of,
And so much more,
You are the key
To my every closed door.

5/1/16

Muse

During those times when I feel so down
Your soothing voice assures me everything is okay
And you lift me up, from the depths of despair

During those thunderstorms and torrential rains
Through the raging thunder and flashes of lightning
I pull you closer to me, in a comforting embrace

During those times when I need to decide
On which path to take, I imagine what you would do
The answer appears, as magically you do

During those times when I don't know what to write
An empty white space gaping blankly at me
I think of you, and the words just flow

During those times when I cheated on you
Pushing you away not acknowledging you are there
You force your way, back into my thoughts

During those nights when I stayed awake, thinking of
you
You took me to those places I've never seen before
And showed me a love that is so real

I always wonder why you look at me so fondly
Even when I've been bad, mad, sad, glad and errant
I wonder why you never cease to love

And why you didn't desert
Even when I proved to be so unworthy
I always wonder why you care

There is no reason why
Since there is nothing I have to give
And there is nothing that you expect

But when I need you, you are always around.
Who are you? Now I now found,
My Muse, my love profound.

10/1/16

5 Words

I want to be like you exactly
And as soon as I get over this.
So Eventually
It's no more or less our fault
Than it is our destiny
How could it be that I'm in ecstasy?
These eyes of mine at once determined
Uncompromising rude reality

11/3/16

Victory or Defeat

Is this victory?
Is this defeat?
If this is victory
Then what's defeat?

It really doesn’t matter folks,
Who wins a savage fight.
Its better far to give a smile,
And then sleep well at night.

Dizzy-eyed fury and great rage of heart
As when, both arms beside her held,
Our laughing little flask, compelled
Suddenly made her from my side to start.

Then again it came across,
Summoned up remembrance of things past,
The sea of all doth lash and toss,
A city in the twilight dim and vast.

With Lying at my heart that beat too fast
Thinking then, writing now when ink has paled
O! Love, thy words have i all availed
Ah! Little thought we 'twas our last!

6/4/16

Marriage

Taken is the word that should be
For its three decades i have passed alone
Truth may seem strange, but cannot be:
I can't just live now on my own.

It's not that, iam not loved
Born in a blessed family, But
Pushed and fallen, fallen and shoved
It's time to get that angel whom i love.

But the road is tough, rugged and rigid
May be the angel can't find her way
She has her own point and say
Strong, Both Bold and Vivid.

She tells me that she loves me
Same is my mutual desire for her
But the swell is strong, violent and harsh
Let the ship sail through it, i did prefer.

Now the wait game has begun
Don't know where it would take
For the skies to clear under the sun
And the ship to sail or blindly to forsake.

So I bought a slice from memory
To relish my new beginning
Life has begun a new game, a new inning.

13/4/16

Beautiful Eyes

You give me peace
In my life span of war
With hopes, hoping flicker and cease
At home in peace, whilst I from far.

Gods do envy us, Cos
We are Mortals
We get to live our life's
While they have to stay put,
At the heavenly portals.

Its again you, my dear,
Analysing an illusion, that
Brings you here.
While these visions did appear.

You talk too less
A good listener though
You should speak your heart out.
Let people might judge them so.

A clear conscience you will have
not to remember talks of lies
Beauty there within your heart
Will sparkle from your beautiful eyes.

6/6/16

Life - Thorns

Pluck a thorn, And
Plant a rose in your heart
Don't think of the past,
Think about the future, a new start.

But he who dares not, grasp the thorn
Should never crave the rose.
When suddenly across the lane
A wind with fingers goes.

Some of the most beautiful things,
Worth having in your life
Come wrapped in a crown of thorns.
He reigns the Jealous God. Who mourns.

I'd rather let you cover all my roads
With thorns, than with dead roses.
For its a life i want to spend with you,
With a thousand fragrant posies.

30/6/16

Stairs To Your Heart

Take my hand
Help me find my way
Of the stairs,
That will lead me to your heart.

The stairs might narrow
But I don't mind at all
As long as I have you
I'll find my way home.

For my home is in your heart
And there's no other place
Like the warmth of your arms
Where true love I found...

So take my hand
Lead me to your arms
There is no other way
But the stairs to your heart...

5/7/16

Don't Judge Me by My Poems

Fathom my thoughts
Try to reach its meaning
Of words I've written
Of this piece I crafted.

Don't be deceived
I might not what you think
Blame my wide wild imaginations
They created things beyond unbelievable...

Just as when I hold my pen
My thought starts to picture a scene
It could be fictional dramatic or romantic
Depending on the mood I could be anything...

Where ever my pen would lead me
I could be in the moon or flying to unknown
I could be a queen romancing a king
Or a beggar begging for food in the street.

I could be a superman fighting with bad men
Or a thief running away from the police
I could be a rose admired by lovers
Or a fish swimming in the deepest sea.

Oh, I could be anything
So don't judge me by the poems I wrote
For nobody could really see

The real identity of a poet
Unless he wants to unfold.

5/7/16

Waves

The waves of the ocean
Are ready to engulf you
But fret not my dear
I won't bid adieu.

Like the continuous waves
Of the ocean, My dear,
My love will last forever
Like the morning dew; clear.

Tic Toc Tic; the time ticks
Continuously like the ocean waves
Better, brighter i see like day
In dark and hidden caves.

Still the waves wants,
to engulf you within.
To stop the storm in the ocean
That passion; yes it did begin.

2/11/16

Wishes and Reality

Wishes of dreams
I wished for
In arms of your love
Lies Heavens and Stars Above

Wishes of Reality
I Never Wished for
To be away from you
Oh Yes! its true

Wishes of Dreams
I wished for
To spend a Life time with you
With vows, Yes I Do.

Wishes of Reality
I Never Wished For
To Yearn for your love
My journey on prey Above.

17/11/16

Unrequited Love

Midnight Memories
Creating a ripple
With a slap
And some tickle

Memories of you
Are Many
Wiping them off
So Grief's not any

Eight Years
Of Love and Care
Wished it till eternity
In a beautiful infinity.

But now its gone
You are no more mine
Tho' love had never
Made us shine.

Unrequited Love
Like rem sleep
In my eyes now
Tears do weep.

Willed Strong
Promised not to cry
Neither love as well
Until i die.

25/5/17

Love

Do you know
That i Still Love You?
It won't be heard
In my silent words
Or would be felt
In my loud gestures.
It's an emotion that
Runs through my heart
Comes like shadows,
And just departs.

7/2/17

Just to see you go Away

I don't intend to hurt you
By the words i say
I fret to lose you, No
Just to see you go away.

You might find it strange
By the words i say now
But its high time to say, now
Or Just see you go away.

Five months i kept my quite
Didn't utter words i should say
Amidst deafening silence, you write, now
I just see you go away.

With silent talks and reading lips
We have in office, many words
I did say, many left unsaid, now
I just see you go away.

Can't express the feelings in words
My heart weeps a silent tear,
Emotions left unsaid, Now
I just see you go away.

13/7/17

I think I know what it is

I think i know what it is
But afraid to admit it
We talk, we chat, we laugh, you cry
It's not worth it, i have explained it, but still WHY?

I think i know what it is
But afraid to admit it
Being the distance though i still can feel your beats
Connected through strings, regardless we meet

I have told you once then
And i say it to you now again
When you're sad and when you're lonely and you
haven't got a friend
Just remember that its not the end

I can feel your beats,
And can sense something's amiss
That's when i asked you today again and again
And offered you a hug though not a kiss

You say you can spend your life with me
Gosh! You have a lot of faith in thee
It's just that i can't see you cry
I can't explain this to myself, WHY?

We count the positives and negatives
The pluses and minuses
Having a gala time, miles apart
Without any booze or any sedative

Just match making for each other
Overlooking a hunch
That we can be together.
It's a thought, a random hunch

I think i know what it is
But afraid to admit it
For its you i feel i have longed since ages
Flipping through time and its countless pages.

I think i know what it is
But afraid to admit it.

8/2/17

A Call at Night

A call at 1.30 in middle of night
Unknown number flashes my cell
In cold dark room with no lights.

Struggling to see the number,
The call was from a distant land.
Sleep in one eye, I almost in slumber.

Then comes a hello, Unknown voice
It seemed at first. Then the choir sings
Lightens my jubilant room with rejoice.

Ages had passed it seemed with no talks
Holocaust escaping from Pandora's
Lead lined box.

Life moved ahead without you, but you did
Move to a distant land, without me even having
A chance to adieu a bid.

Well surprisingly you called in another year
Didn't seem like ages of unspoken words
But happy now to get the mist clear.

You asked me about my poems, Which i stopped
Writing. I felt like a poet with no muse.
Not even a word my pen scribbled, it bluntly refused.

Well a smile on my face after a long time.
Lightened hearts with same long talks
Pen moving in rhyme; with the same old chime.

15/1/17

Rise and fall in love

I used to write poems
And recite them for you over video calls
Just to see your expressions,
Of joys and love; My true confessions.

Though miles away we stayed
Bonding i felt we had
To be with you always you promised
Best times i must say we had.

Then came a true confession
From you which i didn't anticipate
With the peaks and valleys in my life
You gave up on me; didn't even wait.

I felt like i had been used
Like a spare tyre, a Stepney in car
When your life had no air,
You replaced me; I was in to despair!

No hard feeling i have now
Written a last poem for you.
But won't be reciting it over call
'Love' for whose dear love I rise and fall.

26/11/16

Hidden Things

You think they don't hurt,
Those words that you say,
But that's just how it looks.
I've learned to deal with pain,
Though you don't know it.
It kills me inside,
When you say what you say.
I wish i could run and hide,
And that's all you see someone strong,
Not someone weak.
I can't let you know,
How i really feel,
How i cry at night,
When the pains to real.
No matter what you do,
I'll still act the same,
I'll still act strong,
And i'll hide my pain.

27/6/16

Never Meant To be

It was always about we
But we turned to I
Which was never meant to be.

A lesson had to be learnt
Sooner or later
That's its always about I and not We

Together when we were
Everything seemed blissful
But when we turned into I
It was never meant to be

I always question to thy
Was this fate meant for me
From We to I
Which was never meant to be

Though the lesson learnt
After losing blood and fingers burnt
That it had always been about I
Which was never meant to be.

I Want To Enjoy

With smile of sorrow
And Tears of Joy
Its time, I would like to enjoy.

Smile of joy
Tears of sorrow
It's time that, grief's destroy.

Time passes with joy,
Increases with Richness
With a hollow sorry to destroy

Sunrise, Sunset
Joy and Sorrow
I want to smile,
In a Bright Tomorrow

Joy of new
Sorrow of few
I want to smile,
Please! Can i too

Its neither sorrow, nor joy
Either tear or a cry
Its time, I want to enjoy.

2/1/15

Nature

Flowing and happy are lakes and streams
I see them with an eye serene
To be like them is like a dream.

Flying high, a spirited bird
I see them with an eye amaze
To fly like them has always been my craze.

Amidst all, I stand above and tall,
Mountains I see with eyes dazzled
Personality to be like them, baffled.

3/1/15

Distances Apart Miles

It feels great
When you make someone smile
Who is apart from miles
But the one who is apart from miles
Comes close,
What do you call it, Fate!

I'am walking on a sword sharp
One mistake it will split me apart,
Been there, a time not so long ago
To build lost trust
Is like walking on
A mountain covered with snow

My silence speaks for me
But here I would love to speak
To open my mind with you
And scream in silence
Life can be so bleak.

Well here am I
And there you are
Will be with you, though miles apart
Making you smile
With distances miles apart.

4/1/15

Poetry

Poetry
Can strike a chord
Deep within your heart
Which mere words cannot

Poetry
Can stir a wave
Full of emotions
Which mere words cannot.

Poetry
Can set ablaze
Whirlwinds in minds
Which mere words cannot.

9/1/15

The One I Love

Closing the doors
One the ones you love
Is like carrying a burden
To heavy to be true

But at times, you
Need to lighten,
Lighten the weight
Its for a better you.

Love, Time and Wave,
Waits for none
Ups and downs in life
Harsh reality underneath
The bright blue sky

Feeling the excess weight
Carrying on my shoulders
Well, it/s not weight
Its the love I had for you

But with time, wave and surge
I have become strong
Not a single tear, will I shed
While closing the doors on you
The one I Love

9/1/15

Crossroads

I don't know where
life has brought me
It seems like a crossroads
Is it where i'am meant to be

I don't know this place
Never came here before
Everything seems new to me
Its where you, me, we are
Never meant to be

I writers notebook i write now
with prose and verses in it
Mentioning this story here
By each of its pieces and bits

Life has been a roller-coster for me
With bits of joy and ample of struggle
Perhaps it's now too late for the story
It's my crossroads of life
Headed towards a tunnel
Or at a distance
Do i see light?

13/3/15

Distances

It’s in your loneliness
That I would be remembered
But the fact would be, then
I would have gone too far

The distance can't be measured
By miles then
Cos the distances
Is created in my heart

Tried a lot to avoid it
But destiny you call fate
Had played its role
Creating distances in miles first
And then creating it in my heart

I wouldn’t love anyone now
For it takes more than it gives
I should have known this
Forget it, I do know it now.

10/6/15

My Love

Something is wrong with me
I do not know the reason what
Contemplated days for it
Answers left unanswered
Thought I would give it a quit.

Talking to you, you said once
Quitting is easy said, but tough
When done, It not easy to quit
It's difficult when things are left
Undone, when the tide becomes rough.

I started thinking again
What's wrong with me
Something i found amiss
Amidst a diary of half completed poems
It's my love, I found again

My love for poems
I hadn't penned a single poem for days
This was the incompleteness in me
By penning you, you made me complete
In deeper heavens of music
Where night and morning meets

22/6/15

You, Me, We, Never Meant to be

Poetry, a verse of emotions
Tied in knots
Story a prose of thoughts
Fact or fiction, creating an illusion.

Less words more say
Inking my emotions
To write a rhyme
In presence of your absence
In short i would say, mockery of time

Or write a long chapter
For my untitled next
You wouldn't be a chapter though
But the story and the text

Its you and I, turned to we
But you, me, we were
Never meant to be.

29/6/15

Forever Stay Apart

I wish to talk to you
But I won't
It's not a matter of pride
Its cos of love, My Love
That you denied.

I wish to talk a lot
Share my moments with you
Like we did in the recent past
But I won't
It's sad, but true

I wish to talk again
But you know, I won't
Probably you need to start
Rekindle the fire extinguished
Or forever stay apart.

1/7/15

Poetry

Unsaid Emotions turns to poetry
Poetry a mere play of words
Expressed more by saying less
It's the power of Poetry

Read by many
Understood by few
Written by handful
Yet it has the power
To bring Smiles and tears
It's just words you see
Expressions expressed
With no fears

For some it reaches late
For some it reaches on time
Lucky are those for whom
It's being recited
While being written
In a Passionate rhyme.

3/7/15

Dreams

I'am a dream
A dream you see
When you sleep with
Your eyes wide open

A dream, A Mirage
The Cake, The Cream
The Hug, The Kiss,
The Tickle, The Dream

Difficult to get
Yet easy to see
Or waste of time
You hate to regret

I'am a dream
I come in your sleep
Like a secret call
Or like silent tears you weep.

22/7/15

Who Will Not Be Named

I am happy that's its ended
All relations scrapped
Once and for all

You were there
In my dreams and prayers
But now you have lost
That space, As i bade, goodbye

You have fallen
From highest to low
Love will not find a space
In my heart now
You know, and well you know

I don't blame you for it
Neither I'am the one to be blamed
Or the time for the matter
He is the one, who will not be named.

22/7/15

Distances

I had you
Who listened to my poems
As I wrote them along
Though distances there with miles then

Now you don’t even speak
Though distances remains the same, But
Distances now, created in heart

Lack of communication you see
Or may be excess of it
Line you had to draw
Creating a distance somewhere, maybe
Within your heart

Line been drawn, Distances created
But i still write poems
Wanting you to hear, as i wrote
But distances can’t be measured
In miles now, It’s been created
In your heart.

27/8/15

Choices

I need to write a rhyme
For its been quite a while
Life had been colourless
But Intriguing like a mime

For its the high rise that i prefer
Than a massive bungalow
Sitting above listening to the hustle & bustle
Than defaming silence
It's a matter of choices that differs

I like to see the sky lit with fireworks
But now from the ground
It's from high rise above
Gosh! It's the rays of lights, I Love.

19/9/15

Words that has to be Said

Some notes must never be sung
Some Chords must never be struck
Some tunes should be left untouched
Some words should be left unsaid

Words are less, to express
The emotions, unheard, just felt
Writing verses and rhymes
Trying to emote the feelings felt.

Say less, Feel the emotions, they say
How to feel? When emotions are left unsaid.
To say or not to say the emotions you feel,
Say it! As no one knows what lies ahead

Expressed my emotions, result unknown
Screaming silence, through blinding night
Yes or no!, Outcome, i don't know.
Answer, awaited with morning light.

Now, I'am
Singing the perfect tune
Striking the right chords
Melodious the tune now
Saying the words that had to be said.

24/4/15

Closure

Not so very long ago
When you hugged me, We felt the warmth
Hugs to kisses, the gentle touch,
You just played along.

I still can't forget the day
When you came over.
I felt your future, close to your lips,
Combing my hair with your gentle finger tips.

As things progressed,
You seemed freaked out
Daddy's little girl didn't have a choice,
That's what you said with your own voice

It took me time, I did yes move on
Happily married,
Things seemed normal;
Then you again came along.

Regret an Emotion
You had then.
Yearning for my love
You sounded like a mourning dove.

Time moved on, so did you
Excitement on statues you show.
Happy to see you move on as well.
God has answered my prayers i can’t tell.

25/1/2020

About the Author

Academically a Chemical Engineer, Marketer by profession and a writer by hobby can best define the Author Rohit Shetty. Also referred as the Record man of the literary field; Rohit has many National and Internal awards up his name. Prominent of those are

1. Nominated consecutively thrice for India's fourth highest civilian Award 'Padma Shri'
2. 1 Limca Book of Record
3. 2 India Book of Records

Rohit writes in his leisure time, mostly at night when there is utmost silence. He mainly articulates his feeling in form of poetry as he finds it the best way of expression. This is Rohit's 9th Title and 5th Edition of Breaking Silence Series. Other Titles written by Rohit Shetty are

1. Breaking Silence – Poetry
2. Breaking Silence 2 – Poetry
3. Breaking Silence 3 – Poetry
4. Breaking Silence 4 – Poetry
5. Silent Voices – Poetry
6. Mind Games – Self Help
7. Score More – Self Help
8. Murdered To Moksha – Fiction Novel

Just not writing Rohit has also been actively involved in philanthropy work and has been well recognised for it as well. He has been selected as a Mentor Of Change by AIM (Atal Innovation Movement) an initiative by NITI Ayog Government of India. Rohit Shetty has also received prestigious Award of Dr. APJ Abdul Kalam Memorial Excellence - Award for his distinguished services to society and nation.

Rohit Shetty has been instrumental with First Step Publishing to showcase over 200 writers across 35 countries. His title Murdered To Moksha has also received appreciation from India' PM Mr Narendra Modi.

Rohit Shetty has been felicitated twice by MPCC President Mr Manikrao Thackrey and MLC Mr Charan Singh Sapra at the grand finale of the Mulund Festival in 2012 and 2013.

A National Record holder in the field of literary, Rohit writes as a hobby and is currently working in a private company in Mumbai

He can be contacted at rohitnshetty@gmail.com